ETHEL GOES TO THE MARKET

Maite Butron & Brady Ough
Illustrated by Rafael Butron

Ethel Publications
Australia
Copyright © 2019 by Maite Butron & Brady Ough
Illustrations Copyright © 2019 by Rafael Butron

Written by
Maite Butron & Brady Ough

Illustrated by Rafael Butron

Edited by Morgana Willing

ISBN 978-0-6483126-2-8
ISBN 978-0-6483126-3-5   (ebook)

... INTRODUCTION

The Ethel the Echidna series are childrens' books with simple stories that gently show both personal and social boundaries encouraging the healthy development of children.

These stories introduce the practice of mindfulness, emphasizing the importance of awareness about choice when it comes to our behaviour.

ETHEL
GOES TO THE
MARKET
... A PARENTS' GUIDE

This story was designed to address the concepts of managing complicated emotions and meeting individual needs.

Recognising individual needs and explaining appropriate boundaries are fundamental to a child's wellbeing and self-esteem.

Ethel feels physical discomfort and uses this as a cue to pause and unpack her feelings.

By reflecting on her initial response, Ethel considers how her emotions might affect herself and Claudia. Ethel recognises her individual need for alone time and clearly expresses herself. The honest exchange between the two echidnas sets up the opportunity for an authentic relationship.

Ethel the echidna felt excited as she dunked her double bug biscuit into her freshly made tea.

Today was the day of the local market.

Ethel loved wandering
around all by herself.

She always visited
her favourite stalls
and found new treasures
along the way.

Ethel also enjoyed having little chats and jokes with the stall vendors that she met.

Market day was Ethel's time for freedom and exploring.

On the way to the market, Ethel bumped into Jeremy. He was with his cousin Claudia from over yonder hill.

Ethel smiled politely hello then toddled off towards the market.

She was in a hurry.

To her surprise and discomfort, Ethel realised that Claudia had scampered behind her and was now walking beside her.

What was Ethel to do?
Did Claudia want to go
with her?
How would this change
her special day?
What if she didn't want
Claudia to join in?

Ethel felt the heat of discomfort rising inside her chest and thought that she might ignore Claudia.

Maybe she would watch the moth catchers for a while, and just hope that Claudia would leave.

Ethel thought to herself,
no, this simply will not do!
Ethel then noticed that
she was being a little bit
selfish with her thoughts.
So she took three slow
breaths to help herself
think more clearly.

Ethel then turned calmly to Claudia and said, "I'm really sorry Claudia, I don't mean to be rude but I really do enjoy wandering around the market alone, it's my special time to myself."

Claudia smiled and said, "thank you so much for being honest with me Ethel. I feel the same way about going anting, which I think I would prefer to do now anyway."

The two echidnas both
gave a sigh of relief as
they turned to go about
their separate adventures.

The very next week, Ethel was feeling much more comfortable after finding someone she could talk honestly with.

To her own surprise
Ethel invited Claudia
to go to the market
with her.

This time, Ethel enjoyed
showing off her favourite
things. Ethel and Claudia
had a marvellous time and
became very good friends.

On the way home
Claudia showed Ethel
where she had found
some delicious fat ants.

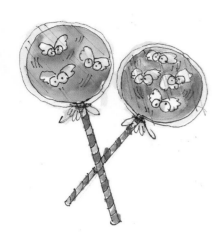

Toffee Ants

This recipe can only be guessed at as it is made by the travelling echidnas deep in the forest and brought to the local markets.

Ingredients:
2 Buckets red gum sap
1 Bucket blossom honey
1 Bucket forest ants
1/2 Bucket fire ants
100 Three hand length sticks - washed and sun dried

Method:

Place a large and heavy pot over red hot coals at the mouth of a rock floored cave beneath light of a full moon.

Bring the red gum sap and blossom honey to a rolling boil. The bubbles will start out large and as the mixture thickens the bubbles become smaller and change in colour from orange to a deep sunset.

Remove from the heat and add all the ants.

Dip each of the one hundred sticks into the thick, ant filled toffee. Be very careful not to burn your claws and spikes as the toffee is very hot.

Swirl each stick one by one until it is about the size of a bulging and swollen eye. Then with a quick and clever movement, place the toffee stick onto the wet rock to cool and set.

Repeat until each of the one hundred sticks have been set down onto the wet rock.

Note: before the sun delivers first light your toffee ant sticks must be collected and ready for market.

Toffee ants are the most popular stall at any market and many believe they hold magical and healing powers.

Double Bug Biscuits

1 Cup ants
1/3 Cup bloodwood honey
1/2 Cup crushed beetles
1/3 Cup ripe quangdong berries
1 Pinch ground cloves
1 Pinch dried cinnamon
1 Cup dried stone ground gum root

Combine the ants, honey, beetles, quangdong berries and spices in a medium sized clay pot.

Stir with small dried branch from an apple tree on a gentle heat.

Remove from coals and allow to cool when the first bubbles appear.

Add the gum root and combine until it feels like stiff mud when the mixture is cool enough that it can be comfortably smeared on your face. (This is a great face mask to ensure a clear and radiant skin).

Roll into balls the size of koala droppings and place on a large cooking stone.

Slide into a hot oven and cook until golden brown.

Cool on a bed of dried gum tree leaves and enjoy..

For Echidnas Only

This story was written by Brady Ough.
He is a parent, grandparent, chef, massage
therapist and energetic healer.

Concept and parenting guide by Maite Butron.
She is a parent and grandparent who works as
a Holistic Counsellor, Relationship Counsellor
and Life Coach.

Both authors are passionate about boundaries
and active, respectful parenting.

Original watercolour drawings by
Rafael Butron, artist and parent.

Edited by Morgana Willing, parent and
early childhood educator.

Recipe inspirations and fun add-ons by
Sofia Hartley.

Design by BA&D.

Eternal gratitude to Ben Jarvis, for
his intellectual and legal guidance.

Printed in Great Britain
by Amazon